CALMING UPSET CUSTOMERS

Rebecca L. Morgan

A FIFTY-MINUTE™ SERIES BOOK

CRISP PUBLICATIONS, INC.
Menlo Park, California

CALMING UPSET CUSTOMERS

Rebecca L. Morgan

CREDITS
Editor: **Tony Hicks**
Designer: **Carol Harris**
Typesetting: **Interface Studio**
Cover Design: **Carol Harris**
Artwork: **Ralph Mapson**

Copyright © 1989 by Crisp Publications, Inc.
Printed in the United States of America

English language Crisp books are distributed worldwide. Our major international distributors include:

CANADA: Reid Publishing Ltd., Box 69559—109 Thomas St., Oakville, Ontario, Canada L6J 7R4. TEL: (905) 842-4428, FAX: (905) 842-9327

Raincoast Books Distribution Ltd., 112 East 3rd Avenue, Vancouver, British Columbia, Canada V5T 1C8. TEL: (604) 873-6581, FAX: (604) 874-2711

AUSTRALIA: Career Builders, P.O. Box 1051, Springwood, Brisbane, Queensland, Australia 4127. TEL: 841-1061, FAX: 841-1580

NEW ZEALAND: Career Builders, P.O. Box 571, Manurewa, Auckland, New Zealand. TEL: 266-5276, FAX: 266-4152

JAPAN: Phoenix Associates Co., Mizuho Bldg. 2-12-2, Kami Osaki, Shinagawa-Ku, Tokyo 141, Japan. TEL: 3-443-7231, FAX: 3-443-7640

Selected Crisp titles are also available in other languages. Contact International Rights Manager Suzanne Kelly at (415) 323-6100 for more information.

Library of Congress Catalog Card Number 88-72256
Morgan, Rebecca L.
Calming Upset Customers
ISBN 0-931961-65-3

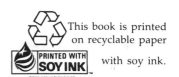

This book is printed on recyclable paper with soy ink.

PREFACE

Customers make or break a business. In many businesses, upset customers are rare. But when a customer is upset, the situation can cause great stress and tension to employees and to other customers. Knowing how to resolve the conflict quickly and professionally can make a big difference in how employees perform their jobs and how customers feel about the organization.

By reading this book and completing the exercises, you will learn:
- Why it's important to calm upset customers
- Why you want customers to complain
- Six things you can learn from upset customers
- Why customers become upset
- What you can do to prevent customers from getting upset
- How your words make a difference
- What the upset customer wants
- How to diffuse defensiveness
- What to do after the customer has left
- What managers need to know about calming upset customers

This book provides practical, easily adaptable ideas that will help you to deal effectively with upset customers in all types of situations.

Rebecca L. Morgan

Rebecca L. Morgan

ABOUT THE AUTHOR

Rebecca L. Morgan is a dynamic professional speaker, seminar leader, and author. Based in San Jose, California, she travels nationally to share her knowledge and experience. In addition to customer satisfaction topics, her presentations cover time management, management communication, and sales training. She is the author of *Professional Selling: Practical Secrets For Successful Sales.* Her clients include Hewlett-Packard, IBM, Apple Computer, Wells Fargo, Macy's, and the American Management Association among many others.

CONTENTS

A Customer Is...

INTRODUCTION
"Upset" Vs "Difficult"   2
Assess Yourself   3
Calming Skills Assessment   4

PART 1:   Why Is it Important to Calm Upset Customers?
Upset Customers Don't Come Back   6
You Want Customers to Complain   7
A Learning Opportunity   8

PART 2:   Why Do Customers Get Upset?
A Customer Could Be Upset Because...   12
Avoidable Upsets   14
Returning Calls   16

PART 3:   What You Can Do
Personal Presentation   20
Nonverbal Communication   22
Words That Make a Difference   25
Watch Your Words   28

PART 4:   Calming Upset Customers
What Do Upset Customers Want?   36
Listening Habits   38
More Words to Watch   40
Additional Pointers   42
Calming Customers Over the Phone   44
Practice   46

PART 5:   After the Customer's Gone
Incident Review   52
Don't Take It Personally or Bore Your Co-Workers   53

PART 6:   Guidelines for Managers
Creating an Environment for Customer Satisfaction   56
Using This Book for a Staff Meeting   58
When Managers Calm Upset Customers   59
Managing Upset Employees   60

PART 7:   Review
What Did We Cover?   64

A CUSTOMER IS...

The most important person to come into this organization
whether in person, on the phone, or by mail.

The person who ultimately pays my paycheck.
I really work for her.

Not someone with whom I should argue. Dale Carnegie said:
"The only way to get the best of an argument is to avoid it"
—especially with customers.

Someone with whom I will learn patience,
even though he is not always patient with me.

Someone who can make or break my day,
depending upon how I react to her comments.
I can easily control my life by controlling
how I respond to situations.

Someone who has biases and prejudices just like I do.
He may not like my hair; I may not like his clothes.
Yet he is a special human being and my customer.

Someone I take care not to offend.
Even when she is wrong, I point out the mistake
indirectly and politely.

Someone who is sometimes a challenge.
I embrace the challenge
and am glad when I can turn a frown into a smile.

Someone who is very special.
She is my customer for a few short minutes
and I focus on serving her needs 100% when I am helping her.

Someone with whom I will go the *"extra mile."*
He may not realize it, but I realize
that the difference between mediocre and excellent
is just 10%.

Rebecca L. Morgan

INTRODUCTION

> If you can keep your head when all about you
> Are losing theirs and blaming it on you . . .
> Yours is the Earth and everything that's on it.
>
> *Rudyard Kipling, "If"*

Wouldn't it be wonderful if there were no upset customers to contend with? But that's not the way the world is. No matter how hard you try, you are bound to come across an upset person once in a while. You need to know how to respond quickly and professionally.

The Win/Win Solution

A recent article in *Nation's Business* quotes Doug Green, founder of New Hope Communications: "We've found that the solution to every problem comes from the spirit of cooperation. I am sure we can come up with something that can make both of us happy, but we must approach this in a very cooperative manner." This book will help you to find those solutions.

Who Should Read This Book?

This book is designed to assist people who deal with the upset public to "keep their heads." The ideas presented here have been useful to people in retail, banking, insurance, medicine, utilities, government, hospitality, travel, manufacturing, and other vocations. These ideas and techniques can be adapted to your job, your personality, and your customers.

"Customers" in this book refers to clients, patients, passengers, ratepayers, taxpayers, homeowners, guests, students, patrons, or any other member of the public that you deal with who ultimately pays your paycheck.

"UPSET" VS "DIFFICULT"

This book will focus on calming *upset* customers who are different from *difficult* customers. When a reasonable person gets upset she may have momentary lapses of unreasonableness, but she is still basically rational and reasonable. But difficult people have a psychological need to get attention by disruptive and negative means. They are chronically hard to communicate with.

Many of the ideas in this book will help you serve difficult people as well as upset people, but there are some people who will be unreasonable no matter what you do. Sometimes you will have to call in your supervisor.

Customers Are Often a Challenge

You can learn from that challenge. The more you learn, the more you'll enjoy your job.

Learning to calm upset people is not easy. There is no single technique that works with every upset person. But there are skills that can be learned, with a positive attitude* and practice.

P.S. The ideas and skills in this book work at home as well.

SELF-ASSESSMENT

---

* For an excellent book on this subject, order *Attitude: Your Most Priceless Possession*, using the information in the back of this book.

ASSESS YOURSELF

Take the following quiz to assess your skills in calming upset customers.

Scoring key: 1=Never, 2=Rarely, 3=Sometimes, 4=Usually, 5=Always		
	NEVER	**ALWAYS**
A. I feel I can calm most upset customers	1 2	3 4 5
B. When I'm with an upset customer, I:		
1. stay calm		1 2 3 4 5
2. don't interrupt		1 2 3 4 5
3. focus on his/her concern without getting distracted		1 2 3 4 5
4. respond to personal accusations without becoming defensive		1 2 3 4 5
5. reduce distractions of paperwork and telephone		1 2 3 4 5
6. have attentive body posture		1 2 3 4 5
7. have appropriate facial expressions		1 2 3 4 5
8. have confident eye contact		1 2 3 4 5
9. listen completely before responding		1 2 3 4 5
10. take notes when appropriate		1 2 3 4 5
11. show empathy		1 2 3 4 5
12. let him/her know I want to help		1 2 3 4 5
13. know when to call on my supervisor		1 2 3 4 5
14. have a confident, helpful tone of voice		1 2 3 4 5
15. use words that don't escalate his/her anger		1 2 3 4 5
16. avoid blaming my fellow workers or company for causing the problem		1 2 3 4 5
C. After the upset customer leaves, I:		
1. am in control of my emotions		1 2 3 4 5
2. don't repeat the story more than once		1 2 3 4 5
3. analyze what I did well and what I'd do differently		1 2 3 4 5

Your Score:

81-100	= Excellent.	21-40	= You may need to ask your supervisor for help.
61-80	= Good.		
41-60	= You need to hone your skills.	1-20	= Start working on this book right now!

To make sure you have a realistic view of skills, photocopy* the following assessment and ask your boss or co-workers to complete it, based on their observations of how you work with upset customers. If their answers are very different from yours, discuss their evaluation with them.

———————

*Permission is granted to photocopy for personal use only, not for classes or other uses.

CALMING SKILLS ASSESSMENT

I'm interested in being the best I can be. I'd like you to candidly assess my skills in calming upset customers, so I can know where to focus my efforts to improve.

Sincerely,

_____

Scoring key: 1=Never, 2=Rarely, 3=Sometimes, 4=Usually, 5=Always

	NEVER		ALWAYS		
A. _____ can calm most upset customers (name)	1	2	3	4	5

B. When _____ is with an upset customer, I believe _____
          (name)   (name)

1. stays calm	1	2	3	4	5
2. doesn't interrupt	1	2	3	4	5
3. focuses on concern without getting distracted	1	2	3	4	5
4. responds to personal accusations without becoming defensive	1	2	3	4	5
5. reduces distractions of paperwork and telephone	1	2	3	4	5
6. has attentive body posture	1	2	3	4	5
7. has appropriate facial expressions	1	2	3	4	5
8. has confident eye contact	1	2	3	4	5
9. listens completely before responding	1	2	3	4	5
10. takes notes when appropriate	1	2	3	4	5
11. shows empathy	1	2	3	4	5
12. lets customer know offered assistance is genuine	1	2	3	4	5
13. knows when to call for help	1	2	3	4	5
14. has a confident, helpful tone of voice	1	2	3	4	5
15. uses words that don't escalate his/her anger	1	2	3	4	5
16. avoids blaming my fellow workers or company for causing the problem	1	2	3	4	5

C. After the upset customer leaves, _____
                                           (name)

1. is in control of emotions	1	2	3	4	5
2. doesn't repeat the story more than once	1	2	3	4	5
3. analyzes what was done well and what needs to be done differently	1	2	3	4	5

Suggestions to help _____ become better with upset customers:
                           (name)

_____

_____

PART 1:

WHY IS IT IMPORTANT TO CALM UPSET CUSTOMERS?

In a survey of service quality conducted by the Financial Institution Marketing Association (FIMA) and Raddon Financial Group, it was discovered that twenty-five percent of customers had expressed a complaint in the previous twelve months. The survey stated, ''In light of this significant percentage, everyone in the organization—from teller to president—must become increasingly aware that he or she is either serving the customer directly or is serving someone in the organization who serves the customer. All positions exist because of the customer.''

Calming upset customers is rarely pleasant, but it must be done. If upset people continue expressing their anger and frustration without intervention, it can upset the whole office.

Why do *you* feel it's important to calm upset customers?

_____

_____

_____

_____

_____

_____

ME? UPSET?

UPSET CUSTOMERS DON'T COME BACK

A recent study showed that customers stop buying from a particular business for the following reasons:

- 1% die (not much you can do about that)
- 3% move away
- 5% form other interests
- 9% for competitive reasons
- 14% due to product dissatisfaction
- 68% *because someone was rude, indifferent, or discourteous to them*

Another survey showed that one out of every five supermarket customers had switched stores in the last 12 months. What made them switch? The way the were treated at the cash registers, mostly.

It is clear that people want and expect good service, and when they are not treated well they don't come back. The FIMA/Raddon study found that in financial institutions, such as banks, " 'Complainers' have an average of 3.2 deposit products. While their problem may involve just one specific product, their entire relationship is in jeopardy over unresolved conflicts."

It can be expensive for your company if your customers decide not to come back. One study found that the average cost of acquiring a new customer was $118.16, yet to keep a current customer happy costs only $19.76. It is six times more expensive to acquire a new customer than to keep a current one. That money could be spent improving your work environment, giving you a raise, or keeping you employed.

Word of Mouth Spreads Quickly

If your organization has a reputation for quick, courteous responses to complaints, people will be more apt to begin their conversation with you rationally. When customers scream and yell it's often because that's what their friend had to do to get some action from your organization.

One study found that, on average, one dissatisfied customer told 11 other people, who each told 5 others. That's 67 (1 + 11 + 55) people spreading bad word-of-mouth about your organization. Most organizations are going to be hurt by that much bad advertising.

YOU WANT CUSTOMERS TO COMPLAIN

Yes, you do. Because if they don't complain they'll just take their business elsewhere, and tell their friends not to do business with you. Think about what happens when you are treated poorly: do you usually complain? Most people don't. They just say "I'm never coming *here* again."

A study conducted by the Technical Assistance Research Program discovered that 96% of a business's customers don't complain when they have a problem. This means that for every complaint the average business receives, there are 24 silent unhappy customers.

Yet if a customer does complain, he is more likely to come back. The act of complaining can actually increase customer loyalty.

Unhappy Customers Who Will Buy From You Again*

No complaint: 37% (63% won't come back)
Complaint not resolved: 46% (54% won't come back)
Complaint resolved: 70% (30% won't come back)
Complaint resolved *quickly*: 95% (only 5% won't come back)

* % customers with major cause for complaint (over $100 losses) who will buy from you again.

So remember: Encourage customers to complain when they have a problem.

YOU MEAN A B.L.T. IS NOT
A BLUEBERRY LEMON TART?

A LEARNING OPPORTUNITY

We can learn from every experience, if we choose. Even a difficult encounter can be an opportunity to learn something new, or to apply what you've learned. What can you learn from dealing with upset customers?

I can learn:

_____

_____

_____

_____

_____

_____

What You Can Learn!

You don't ever want to complain like that. Isn't anger ugly, when expressed inappropriately?

Patience. It takes a lot of patience to listen attentively to someone while they are yelling.

What specific company procedures or practices may be annoying your customers. Then you can work to change these.

There may be something in your behavior that irritates people. You can work at changing this.

To show confidence. People can tell if you are confident in your skills or not. An irate person is more apt to hassle someone who appears unsure of himself.

How to calm upset people. You get to practice your calming skills.

> Richard Bach, in his book *Illusions* wrote: ''You are never given a problem without a gift for you in its hands.'' We are given gifts in these upset people.

SUMMARY

In the Introduction section we looked at why it is important to calm upset customers, and to actually solicit complaints from unhappy customers.

Now apply these ideas to *your* work situation. Why is it important for you to calm upset customers?

_____

_____

_____

_____

_____

_____

Why is it important for you to encourage unhappy customers to complain?

_____

_____

_____

_____

_____

_____

PART 2: WHY DO CUSTOMERS GET UPSET?

Customers become upset for various reasons. Sometimes their anger is justified; sometimes it's not. Either way, in working to resolve their upset it helps to know what caused the upset.

Why do you think customers get upset? Write 3–5 responses in the space provided, then compare your answers with items listed on the next page.

_____

_____

_____

_____

_____

_____

WELL YES, MADAME... BUT WE **DID** REMOVE THE STAIN.

A CUSTOMER COULD BE UPSET BECAUSE...

- She has expectations that have not been met.
- He was already upset at someone or something else (his boss, his spouse, his kids, a co-worker, other business).
- She's tired, stressed, or frustrated.
- He feels like a victim—not much power in his life in general.
- She feels that no one will listen to her unless she yells and makes a ruckus.
- He will use any excuse to prove he is right, whether he is or not.
- She walks around with a chip on her shoulder—nothing is right in her life.
- You or someone in your organization promised him something that was not delivered.
- You or someone in your organization was indifferent, rude, or discourteous to her.
- He was told one thing by one staff member and something else by another.
- She acted on something told her by a staff member and it was wrong.
- He feels you or someone else in your organization had an unpleasant attitude toward him.
- She doesn't feel she was listened to.
- Prejudices—he may not like your hair, clothes, makeup, etc.
- She feels she can manipulate you to get what she wants if she makes a lot of noise.
- He's suspicious of your organization and thinks your organization or you are dishonest.
- She made a wrong assumption about what your organization would do for her.
- He was told he has no right to be angry.
- She was given a smart or flip reply.
- He was transferred on the phone without his consent.
- She was screened on the telephone.
- He is embarrassed at doing something incorrectly.
- Her integrity or honesty has been questioned.
- You or someone in your organization argued with him.
- You don't have enough job training to handle their situation quickly and accurately.

UPSET PEOPLE HAVE LITTLE PATIENCE

Annoyances that a person usually tolerates become intolerable when that individual is upset.

You can't control another person's behavior. But you can change *your* behavior to avoid causing annoyance.

Look again at the reasons why customers get upset. Which ones do you have any control over? List those you feel that you at least partially can control and briefly note what your control is in the space below:

Reasons Customers Become Upset	Action I Can Take To Help

AVOIDABLE UPSETS

The annoyances you have some responsibility for causing are:

You or someone in your organization promised something that was not delivered.

> If you promised the customer you would get back to him and you didn't, then he may become upset. With good reason. Most of us become upset when people promise action and don't follow through.

You or someone in your organization was indifferent, rude, or discourteous to her.

> Many times discourtesy is unintentional. You may not have thought about your statement before you blurted it out. Some people try to make funny comments, but these may come across as rude. Treat every customer as you would a special aunt or uncle.

He feels you or someone else in your organization had an unpleasant attitude toward him.

> Perhaps this customer was surly himself, dressed unusually, or treated you poorly. This is no excuse for you to react unprofessionally.

She doesn't feel she was listened to.

> People want to be listened to. They don't want to have to repeat themselves.

He was told he has no right to be angry.

> Everyone has a right to their emotions. Telling them otherwise is sure to make them even angrier.

She was given a smart or flip reply.

> Sarcastic remarks only heighten anger, they seldom ease tension.

AVOIDABLE UPSETS (Continued)

He is embarrassed at doing something incorrectly.

Make sure the customer understands what he needs to know before he tries to use your product or service. Go over any procedures about returns or guarantees before hand. That way you'll have fewer customers who are angry because of a misunderstanding.

Her integrity or honesty has been questioned.

Treat customers with respect and dignity. If there is a problem, assume your organization has made the mistake until shown otherwise. Instead of ''You didn't pay us,'' say, ''We don't have a record of receiving your payment. Would you be kind enough to see if your check cleared the bank?''

Work to eliminate body language, voice tone, or facial expressions that convey distrust. Avoid projecting an ''us versus them'' attitude about customers.

Never call a customer a deadbeat, liar, cheat, thief, etc. Never threaten a customer.

You or someone in your organization argued with the customer.

As Dale Carnegie said; ''The only way to get the best of an argument is to avoid it.'' This is especially true with customers. If you argue with a customer you always lose—even if you win the argument. It's not good for the other customers to witness an argument. They won't like seeing you treat a customer poorly, whether or not the customer was in the wrong.

RETURNING CALLS

Following up on the information you promised is one way you can avoid receiving upset callers or visitors. Even if you have to call a customer back to say you're still checking, she'll appreciate knowing that you haven't forgotten and are doing your best.

The facing page contains a simple form you can duplicate* to keep on top of the follow-up responses you promised. If you have customers in different time zones, this will help you remember to call them back during their work day. Keep this form in front of you to remind you of what you've promised.

CALLBACK SCHEDULE

	NAME	PHONE #	REGARDING
before 8:00			
before 9:00			
before 10:00			
before 11:00			
before 12:00			
before 1:00			
before 2:00			
before 3:00			
before 4:00			
before 5:00			

PART 3: WHAT YOU CAN DO

In Part 3 we will look at what you can do to avoid turning a dissatisified customer into an angry one. We will see the importance of:

- Personal Presentation
- Nonverbal Communication
- Words That Make a Difference

PERSONAL PRESENTATION

One of the things that can irritate an already upset person is your personal presentation. If he feels your grooming and dress are unprofessional or inappropriate, he is more likely to hassle you.

Here are some areas of personal presentation which, if not seen to, may have a negative influence on an upset person.

Check to make sure your
- hair is clean, brushed or combed, and well kept
- makeup is applied neatly, moderately, and appropriately
- clothing is pressed, neat, clean, and in good repair
- hands and fingernails are clean, no chipped polish
- face is shaved or moustache/beard is neatly trimmed
- stockings are run-free
- breath is fresh

Anything else you can think of?
- _____
- _____

How can your personal presentation affect how an upset customer reacts to you?

_____

_____

_____

_____

_____

_____

_____

FIRST IMPRESSIONS

We all make assessments of others, and initially those assessments are based mainly on personal presentation. Some experts claim we make decisions about people within the first four seconds of our meeting them.

> Bay Alexander, President of Professional Impact in Santa Cruz, California says:
>
> If you are in a position where you are likely to interact with angry customers you have a chance to use your image as one of your more effective tools. You can use your image to signal your power, control, knowledge, and composure. If you are dressed inappropriately or too casually for your position and business, customers are more likely to push to get their way, and call for a higher authority if they don't like your response.

You may have experienced the power of your appearance when *you* are a customer. Have you noticed how much easier it is to return an item to a store when you are neatly dressed than when you wear torn jeans and a dirty teeshirt?

***YOU NEVER GET A SECOND CHANCE TO MAKE
A FIRST IMPRESSION***

NONVERBAL COMMUNICATION

Here are some ways your body language and voice tone may have an influence on an upset person:

► Facial Expression

When people complain, do you ever roll your eyes?
Do you scowl?
Do you have an inappropriate smile?

Be aware of your facial expression when you communicate. Ask friends, co-workers, and your supervisor whether you have facial expressions that could be annoying, especially to upset customers.

You want to have a calm, concerned, sincere, interested facial expression. You want to show the customer you care.

Some people smile when they are tense, but don't smile while a customer is expressing anger. If you do, the customer may feel that your not taking her seriously.

► Body Posture

Do you loll on your desk/work area?
Do you slouch?

Show you are attentive to your customer by standing and sitting up straight. When you loll or slouch you may seem inattentive or disinterested.

Maintain a nonthreatening, open body posture. Stand far enough away to give the customer room. Don't crowd him—this may increase his irritation.

► Movement

Do you move slowly when you have to find something for the upset customer?

Upset customers want to see you respond to their needs speedily. This doesn't mean you have to sprint to help, but don't mosey either.

► Gestures

Do you stand/sit with your arms crossed?
Do you hold your head up with your hand/s?

The most common interpretation of the arms-crossed gesture is that the person is closed and unwilling to listen. When communicating with an upset customer, uncross your arms to show you are listening and have an open mind.

► Smoking

Don't smoke in front of customers, even if your employer allows you to smoke in your work area. Always put the cigarette out, even if your customer is smoking.

► Touching

Avoid touching an upset person, especially if he appears potentially violent. This could set off his violence.

► Chewing Gum or Eating

Don't chew gum or eat when you've on the phone or in the public eye. Even if your employer allows it, these acts can be annoying, and can escalate an upset customer into an irate one.

► Voice Tone

Your attitude is projected through your voice as well as your body language. Remember, helping customers is your job, and if you can't stand to help upset people, get transferred to another job. Make sure your attitude is always ''I'm here to help as best I can.''

>   Do you sound annoyed?
>   Does your voice go up at the end of a statement?

People respond more to *how* you say something than to *what* you say. When your voice is annoyed, impatient, or condescending, the customer will become more angry. When your voice sounds confident she will believe you know what you're talking about and it will be easier to calm her.

When your voice goes up at the end of a sentence it sounds as if you're asking a question. Listen to yourself in a tape recorder and hear if your voice goes up at the end. If so, practice having an even tone, or one that ends on a lower note. You will sound confident and *competent*.

Speak with a calm, firm, caring, soothing tone.

► Sighing

Sighing often suggests annoyance or impatience. Don't sigh in front of an upset customer.

► Cursing

Even if the customer curses, there is never an excuse for you to curse. No matter how many insults he shouts at you, remember that you are a professional. Compose yourself as best you can, and avoid responding to abuse.

It is a sign of strength, not weakness, to stay calm and respond with patience when someone is cursing and insulting you.

SELF-ASSESSMENT

What are the areas which *you* need to work at improving?

I need to:

Body Language

Facial expression _____

Body posture _____

Movement _____

Gestures _____

Smoking _____

Touching _____

Chewing gum or eating _____

Voice Tone _____

Sighing _____

Cursing _____

WORDS THAT MAKE A DIFFERENCE

The words you use with customers can help communication or they can start a fight. Here are some common Fight Starters and some suggestions on replacing them with Communication Helpers.

Keep it Impersonal

Fight Starter:

    You didn't do this right.

Communication Helper:

    There are a few areas on this form that we need to complete.

If the customer did something wrong, point out the mistake indirectly. She will often be embarrassed at her mistake. She may get angry because of this embarrassment and try to blame you.

Avoid statements that are sarcastic, blaming, or condescending. Even if the customer is wrong, the time to make it known is not during a rage.

Use "I" instead of "you"

Fight Starter:

    You're wrong.

Communication Helper:

    I can see there's been a miscommunication.

Fight Starter:

    You're confusing me.

Communication Helper:

    I'm confused.

Don't blame the customer. When explaining what went wrong, use either the indirect approach or "I" statements as much as possible.

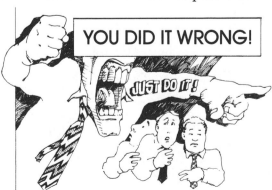

WORDS THAT MAKE A DIFFERENCE (Continued)

Here are some more Fight Starters and Communication Helpers.

Avoid Giving Orders

Fight Starter:

You *have to...*

Communication Helper:

Will you...please!
It would be best if we...

People don't like to be given no choice. Ask them pleasantly to do something or explain how it will be to their benefit.

People don't like to be given orders. Rephrase it more politely as a question. Indirect orders.

Fight Starter:

You *should have* done it this way.

Communication Helper:

We want your next visit to go as smoothly as possible. This will assist you.

Fight Starter:

Wait here

Communication Helper:

Would you mind waiting while I speak to my supervisor?

When people hear ''should'' they often think of their parents or some other authority figure telling them what they did wrong. Instead of telling them what they *should* have done last time, tell them what will be helpful for next time. The past is past and there's nothing anyone can do about it. Focus on the future—the next time—instead.

Take Responsibility

Tell the customer what he and you can do, not what can't be done.

Fight Starter:

I *can't...*

Communication Helper:

I don't have the authority. However, Mary should be able to help you.
Let me get her.
You can...

If you cannot help, connect the customer with someone who can.

Fight Starter:

It's not my job.

Communication Helper:

Let me see what I can do to help.
John is the specialist in that area. Let me get him for you.

Even if what the customer needs isn't within your job duties, never tell her that. Tell her how you can help.

WORDS THAT MAKE A DIFFERENCE (Continued)

If people think they're being criticized, they'll react defensively—that is, angrily.

Avoid Causing Defensiveness

Fight Starter: *Communication Helper:*

    You *never* do it right.   This is often not done correctly.

    You're *always* late.   This payment is often late.

"Always" and "never" sound critical and uncompromising, use "often" instead.

Fight Starter: *Communication Helper:*

    You filled this out okay, *but*. . .   You filled this out well, and. . .

People don't listen to what you say before the "but;" they concentrate on what follows. Use "and" instead, so they'll listen to the whole sentence.

Fight Starter: *Communication Helper:*

    It will *cost* you. . .   The rate is. . .

"Cost" sounds negative, and costs can imply time, aggravation, and other things in addition to money.

Fight Starter:

    What's your *problem?*

                     Communication Helper:

                     Please tell me what happened.

People don't like to have problems, and they don't like others to know they have problems. Use the communication helper instead.

WATCH YOUR WORDS

You can see how important it is to choose the right words and show a positive, helpful attitude. How would you respond in these situations? Check your responses with the author's on page 32.

1. **Customer:** "Can you put this sweater on hold for me?"
   Staff: "I can only hold it until closing."

Why wouldn't you say this to a customer? _____

_____

How would you rephrase the response? _____

_____

2. **Customer:** "I would like to be on the preferred customer mailing list."
   Staff: "You have to have spent $1000 or more."

Why wouldn't you say this to a customer? _____

_____

How would you rephrase the response? _____

_____

3. **Customer:** "Why haven't I received my refund?"
   Staff: "Because you filled in the form all wrong."

Why wouldn't you say this to a customer? _____

_____

How would you rephrase the response? _____

_____

WATCH YOUR WORDS (Continued)

4. **Customer:** "Do you have mittens?"
   Staff: "You'll have to go to accessories for that."

Why wouldn't you say this to a customer? _____

_____

How would you rephrase the response? _____

_____

5. **Customer:** "Are there any more of these forms?"
   Staff: "I don't think so."

Why wouldn't you say this to a customer? _____

_____

How would you rephrase the response? _____

_____

6. **Customer:** "How can I get hold of Dr. Jackson?"
   Staff: "Call her."

Why wouldn't you say this to a customer?

_____

How would you rephrase the response?

_____

WATCH YOUR WORDS (Continued)

7. **Customer:** ''I'm not sure where to submit these forms.''
   Staff: ''Here. Look it up yourself.''

Why wouldn't you say this to a customer? _____

_____

How would you rephrase the response? _____

_____

8. **Customer:** ''I was billed for these PE clothes and I never checked them out.''
   Staff: ''You must have, otherwise you wouldn't have been billed for them.''

Why wouldn't you say this to a customer? _____

_____

How would you rephrase the response? _____

_____

9. **Customer:** ''How do I get to the Shamrock Room?''
   Staff: ''There's a map over there.''

Why wouldn't you say this to a customer? _____

_____

How would you rephrase the response? _____

_____

WATCH YOUR WORDS (Continued)

10. **Customer:** "Why do I need to give you I.D.? I've been banking here for years."
    Staff: "It's bank policy."

Why wouldn't you say this to a customer? _____

_____

_____

How would you rephrase the response? _____

_____

11. **Customer:** "Can you open a new account for me?"
    Staff: "You'll have to wait for the New Accounts person."

Why wouldn't you say this to a customer? _____

_____

_____

How would you rephrase the response? _____

_____

*THIS CAN HAPPEN IF YOU
DON'T WATCH YOUR WORDS*

WATCH YOUR WORDS—Authors Suggested Responses

The following are the author's suggested responses to the previous situation on pages 28-31.

1. This response is negative. Rephrase it as a positive response:

   ''Yes, I'd be glad to hold it until closing time tonight, which is 6:00.''

2. Again, this is the negative. It assumes that the customer doesn't qualify.

   Rephrase it without the negative assumption:

   "I'd be delighted to add you to the list. This list is for customers who meet the qualification of having spent $1000 with us this year. Does that qualification fit for you?"

3. This response will make the customer feel embarrassed, and probably angry. Rephrase it to make it less personal:

   ''I'm sorry for the delay. It seems that the form was not completed correctly. I'll help you put it right.''

4. It doesn't answer the question. Also, it sounds like an order. Rephrase it to *invite* the customer to visit the Accessories Department, instead of saying he has to:

   ''Yes, we do carry mittens. There's a wide selection in our Accessories Department, which is at the top of those stairs.''

5. This response is not very helpful. Rephrase it to offer some assistance to the customer:

   ''Let me check for you.''

6. This is a flip response to a serious question. Rephrase it to give the information she asked for:

   ''You can call her during her office hours, Mondays, Wednesdays, and Fridays, between two and four, at 555-1212, or drop in on her during those times in Room 733, or drop her a note in her mail box in Room 345. Let me write that down for you.''

AUTHORS SUGGESTED RESPONSES (Continued)

7. The staff person is giving an order rather than offering assistance. Rephrase it to be more helpful:

   "I'm not sure. Let's look it up in this book. Here it is. It says you can give them to the Admissions Clerk. He's right down this hall, in Room 745."

8. The staff person is calling the customer a liar. Rephrase it without the accusation:

   "I'm sorry for the confusion. Let me pull your records so we can see what happened and fix it. What's your last name, please?"

9. Not very helpful, is it? Give the information asked for:

   "It's down this hall, then take a left and you'll see it straight ahead."

10. Customers don't want to hear "It's policy." Explain how this policy is a benefit to the customer:

    "We ask for two I.D.'s for your protection. I'm sure many other bank personnel know you, Mr. Perez. I'm new here so I want to make sure I'm not giving your money to someone who says he's you and isn't."

11. Answer the question without telling the customer what she has to do:

    "We'd be glad to have your new account. Ms. Firestone, our New Accounts Officer, can set up your new account for you. She'll be available in just a few minutes. Won't you please have a seat? I'll let her know you're waiting."

PART 4: CALMING UPSET CUSTOMERS

In Part 3 we discussed how your personal presentation, body language, voice tone, and choice of words can irritate upset customers. Once the customer is angry—for whatever reason—you need some techniques for calming him down. In Part 4 we'll look at:

> - What Do Upset Customers Want?
> - Listening Habits
> - More Words to Watch
> - Additional Pointers
> - Calming Customers over the Phone

WHAT DO UPSET CUSTOMERS WANT?

Upset customers may want a variety of responses from you:
- to be taken seriously
- to be treated with respect
- to get immediate action
- to gain compensation/restitution
- to have the party who wronged them reprimanded and/or punished
- to clear up the problem so it never happens again
- to be listened to

BUSINESS THRIVES WHEN EMPLOYEES LISTEN

THE CUSTOMER WANTS...

To be taken seriously

The customer does not want a response like ''You're kidding,'' ''No way'' or ''You've got to be joking.'' He wants you to be professional and confident and to respond seriously to his concern.

To be treated with respect

The upset person doesn't want condescension or arrogance. She wants you to treat her and her concern with respect. This may be difficult when the customer is clearly at fault but is trying to blame your organization.

Immediate action

He doesn't want you to look into it next month, next week, or even tomorrow. He wants you to do something *now*. Show you are concerned by moving briskly, no matter how tired you are.

Compensation/restitution

He wants someone to pay for the damage done, and perhaps for his time, inconvenience, or pain.

Someone to be reprimanded and/or punished

Assure the customer that corrective action will be taken, even if you aren't the supervisor. Discreetly report the incident to the supervisor so she can explain the problem to your co-worker and avoid similar problems in the future.

To clear up the problem so it never happens again

Sometimes the customer just wants to know that some action has been put in motion, so that no one will have this problem again. Assure her you will report the problem to the person who can take care of it.

To be listened to

What the upset customer wants first is to be listened to. It is difficult to listen carefully in a tense situation, especially if you have not developed effective listening habits.

Why don't we listen well? What habits do you think prevent people from listening fully, especially in stressful situations?

_____

_____

_____

*For an excellent book on listening, *The Business of Listening*, see the back of this book.

LISTENING HABITS

According to Dr. Lyman K. Steil, President of Communication Development, in St. Paul, Minnesota, most people have poor listening habits. Some of the habits Dr. Steil has discovered are:

► Criticizing the speaker and delivery

Focusing not on what the speaker is saying, but how she is saying it. Noticing a lisp, a stutter, an accent, a dialect, grammatical errors, ''uns'' and ''uhs''—rather than the speaker's thoughts and feelings.

► Listening only for facts and not for feelings

A customer may not *say* he's angry, but his voice conveys it loudly and clearly. Listen carefully for emotions as well as facts.

► Not taking notes—or trying to write down everything

Not taking notes can cause problems later, when you try to remember what was said. On the other hand, trying to take down everything the customer says will make you lose all eye contact. Take a few brief notes of important details, like dates, times, amounts, and account numbers.

► Faking attention

Customers can quickly discern if you are paying attention to them or not. If she was mildly agitated before, your inattention can push her into anger. Pay close attention when you are helping her.

► Tolerating or creating distractions

Don't be distracted by other's conversations. Work at eliminating visual distractions by removing paper piles and pulling out a clean piece of paper to take notes. Listen fully to the customer and eliminate whatever distractions you can.

► Tuning out difficult or confusing information

When people are upset they don't always communicate clearly. If you habitually tune out what you don't immediately understand, practice pleasantly asking the person to slow down. It's easier to understand information one piece at a time. Take notes to help you put the pieces together.

LISTENING HABITS (Continued)

► Letting emotional words block the message

The upset customer may call you names, curse, or say unpleasant things about you, your co-workers, and your organization. Avoid letting him "push your buttons" in this way, because when you're upset you've lost objectivity, and you need to be in control if you're going to find a solution to this situation.

► Interrupting or finishing the other person's sentences

This is an irritating habit and will only induce more anger in an already upset person.

► Biases and prejudices

We all have biases and prejudices, whether we like to admit it or not. You may not like the way someone dresses, her makeup, his hair style, or her stutter. It is hard to listen when you're distracted by these biases. Work on eliminating your prejudices so as to be a better listener.

► Not facing the upset person

Look her in the eye. Remember what your parents said when you were a kid: "Look at me when I'm talking to you." People see you are listening when you are looking at them.

► Not checking that you've understood

Repeat what you understand the customer to be saying. Start your sentence with "Let's see if I understand . . ." or "I think I understand . . . (then paraphrase what she said). Don't say "What you're trying to say is . . ."—it implies the customer is an idiot and can't say what he means. Also avoid "What I hear you saying is . . ."—it's overused and trite.

MORE WORDS TO WATCH

In the last chapter, we looked at words that can be annoying and words that are more neutral—Fight Starters and Communication Helpers. Here are some more words to avoid—because they'll enrage someone who's already upset—and alternatives that will help to calm the person down.

Use verbal cushions—show empathy

Verbal cushions let the customer know that you can understand why she would be upset. You're not saying you know exactly how she feels, because you can't know that.

You're also acknowledging his right to feel that way. You're not pooh-poohing his feelings.

Fight Starters:	*Communication Helpers:*
You're crazy.	I can appreciate what you're saying.
I know how you feel.	I can undersand how you'd feel that way.
	I can understand how that would be annoying.
Boy, you're sure mad.	I can see how you'd be upset.
I don't know why you're so upset.	I would be upset too.
	It sounds as if we've caused you inconvenience. I'm sorry.

Use the 3 F's: Feel, Felt, Found

The 3 F's are a skeleton on which to hang the rest of your response. This technique acknowledges the customer's feelings and offers an explanation in a way she can listen to:

''I understand how you could feel that way.
Others have felt that way too.
And then they found, after an explanation, that this policy protected them, so it made sense.''

MORE WORDS TO WATCH (Continued)

Get clarification

Paraphrase what he is saying. Take the blame if there is a miscommunication. Make sure you understand the concern before you try to solve it.

Fight Starters:

You're way off base.

You aren't making any sense.

That's definitely wrong.

Did you really say...

Communication Helpers:

What it sounds like you're saying...

Maybe I misunderstood...

Let me see if I've got this straight...

Here's what I understood you to say...

Form a team

Let her know her patronage is important. When you form a team it is the two of you together working on a solution, rather than Her vs. You.

Fight Starters;

We can't do that.

You sure have a problem.

Communication Helpers:

I want to help find a solution.

Let's see what we can work out together.

***TEAMWORK IS BETTER THAN WORKING
ALONE ON A PROBLEM***

ADDITIONAL POINTERS

► Time Out

If you find yourself becoming upset, wanting to cry, or to yell at the customer, allow yourself a little time away from the situation. This will give you a chance to calm down before you return to the fray.

When you know you're getting emotional, excuse yourself politely:

> ''Excuse me a moment while I check the policy on this.''
> ''I'd like to get my supervisor's opinion on this.''
> ''I need to verify some information in the file.''
> ''I need to discuss how we can best solve this. I'll be just a moment.''

Always excuse yourself in a way that shows your interest in serving the customer.

► Crying

Upset customers can say things that are hurtful, often without realizing that you may take their comments personally. Whatever you do, don't cry in front of the customer. If your emotions take over, you cannot be as professional as you need to be.

If you find yourself beginning to cry, excuse yourself, and go to an empty office, the rest room, or a back room so you can compose yourself undisturbed. If you don't feel you can bear talking with the customer, ask one of your colleagues or your boss to take over.

► How to Get the Customer's Attention

If the customer is ranting and not giving you a chance to explain or ask questions, use his or her name at the beginning of your sentence. Most people listen when they hear their name.

► If The Customer Is Obstinate...

If you are having trouble reaching an agreement, make comments that direct the customer toward finding a solution:

> "What would you like me to do now?"
> "What do you think is a fair way to settle this?"
> "What would make you happy?"

Often, what she will ask for is less than you might have offered. If the customer's proposal is within your guidelines, accept it. If not, make a counterproposal.

If you can't reach an agreement, it's time to call in your boss. Unless you are a manager, it is not your place to invite a customer to take her business elsewhere.

► Polite Repetition

If the customer keeps insisting on something that's unreasonable or impossible, tell them what you can do (not what you can't do). Keep repeating it, without becoming hostile or loud, until you're finally heard. For example, if the customer insists on getting a widget, and you have none in stock, the conversation might go like this:

> "I want my widget today."
> "I'm sorry, we will have more widgets in on Tuesday."
> "But I need it today."
> "I'm sorry, we don't have any in stock."
> "I want it today."
> "I'll be glad to get one to you on Tuesday."

Eventually, you may have to ask him to leave. If he won't, then call in the security guards or the police.

► Dealing with Violence

There may be occasions when an enraged customer threatens you, or becomes violent. Rely on your gut feeling if it seems things are getting out of hand. Learn to look for potentially violent behavior by reading the nonverbal communication of the customer—clenched fists, tight lips, agitated tone of voice, tense body posture, flared nostrils, red face, and wide-open eyes. Look for evidence of drugs or alcohol.

If the customer becomes unruly, or threatens violence, seek assistance. You do not have to put up with threats.

Never try to reason with a drunk or a drug user. Even if there's no sign of drugs, if the person appears potentially violent, don't feel stupid about calling the police. There are plenty of stories about employees being punched by upset customers. It's better to risk feeling stupid than to end up in the hospital.

Never accuse a customer of being drunk or on drugs. This can put you and your company in a liable situation. Find another way to assist the customer out of your establishment.

CALMING CUSTOMERS OVER THE PHONE

It is easier for a customer to be abusive on the phone because you are a faceless representation of the organization. The guidelines we've discussed throughout this book generally apply when calming customers on the phone. There are a few areas you'll need to modify, however.

Because there is no face-to-face contact, communicating over the telephone presents special challenges. One study by Dr. Albert Mehrabian found that our first impression of someone is made up of 55 percent visual cues (e.g., body language), 38 percent vocal (e.g., tone of voice), and only 7 percent verbal (e.g., words). One expert estimated that this percentage changes to 82 percent vocal and 18 percent verbal when we communicate over the telephone.

You can see how critical it is that your voice tone be pleasant, concerned, patient, informed, and caring. When a customer cannot see your concerned face, she needs to hear concern in your voice. It also helps to deepen your telephone voice. Lower voices are perceived as being more mature, confident, and in control.

There are several ways to see if you have a good voice tone. One way would be to get feedback from your boss or a co-worker. It must be someone who will be honest with you, yet offer feedback caringly, or you could record yourself. Even though your voice on tape sounds different to you than you think it should, this is an excellent way to hear how others hear you.

You could still be annoying customers, even if your voice is pleasant. You may have irritating habits, such as gum chewing, eating, covering the receiver to talk to co-workers, or leaving the customer on hold too long.

If you need to leave the line during a call, ask the customer if she'd rather be called back or put on hold. If she prefers to be called back, tell her you'll call her by a certain time, and ask if that's acceptable. Call back at the agreed time, even if you've nothing to report except that you're still working on it.

If he prefers to be kept on hold, explain that it may be several minutes before you'll have the information. Give him your name in case he decides to hang up and needs to call again. And ask for his number in case you get disconnected.

This kind of service shows the customer that she really matters, and that your organization is run by thoughtful, helpful *people*, not cold computers.

STEP-BY-STEP GUIDELINES

When you're dealing with an upset customer:

1. Verbally cushion the customer's concerns.
2. Use the 3 F's.
3. Apologize for the situation.
4. State you want to help.
5. Probe for more information.
6. Repeat their concern to make sure you've understood.
7. Show you value their patronage.
8. Explain options or ask what they'd like to have happen.
9. Summarize actions to be taken—yours and theirs.
10. End pleasantly.

Throughout:

Listen.

Face the customer.

Look him/her in the eye.

Adopt a concerned body posture, voice tone, and facial expression.

Avoid Fight Starters.

Avoid a condescending or impatient tone.

Have and show empathy.

Eliminate distractions.

Practice patience.

Use a pleasant tone of voice.

Don't take things personally.

PRACTICE

Here are some situations you might encounter in your organization. They won't exactly match your situations, but they may be similar.

Write your responses in dialogue form—what you would actually say, not a description of the scene. Then ask a co-worker to role-play these scenes with you aloud and give each other feedback.

Example:

Customer (to bank teller): "You have sent me someone else's cancelled checks *again*. I have had it. I want to close my account right now."

Teller: "I'm sorry about the mistake and I can understand your concern. If you'll give me your account number I'll get you the correct checks immediately. We'd hate to lose you as a customer."

Now write your responses. Then compare your responses with those on page 49.

1. Customer: "I have waited in line for twenty minutes. What takes you people so long?"

_____

_____

_____

_____

_____

PRACTICE (Continued)

2. ''You made a mistake again on my bill. My records say I owe $62.00 and your statement says I owe $323.50. I want you to fix it. Can't you people do anything right?''

_____

_____

_____

_____

_____

3. ''Your service has been totally unsatisfactory. You promised to deliver my widget three weeks ago and I haven't heard from anyone since. I want it delivered—today.''

_____

_____

_____

_____

4. ''You have done this completely wrong. You are incompetent. I want to see your supervisor immediately so I can have you fired.''

_____

_____

_____

_____

PRACTICE (Continued)

5. ''Your manager has been letting me do it this way for years. Even though she isn't in today, why don't you just let me do it this way so I can stop wasting my time here?''

_____

_____

_____

_____

_____

6. Write a scenario that has happened to you that you felt uneasy dealing with. Write the customer's part as well as your own. Write how you would respond now, after reading this book.

Customer: _____

_____

_____

_____

Your response: _____

_____

_____

_____

_____

SUGGESTED RESPONSES TO PRACTICE EXERCISES

1. ''I can understand how you'd be upset. You've waited a long time. I'll help you get through your transaction quickly. How can I help you now?''

2. ''I'm sorry your account doesn't balance. Let me research your account transactions and see what went wrong so we can make sure it doesn't happen again. May I have your account number, please?''

3. ''I can understand why you'd be upset. I would be too. I'm sorry your widget hasn't been delivered. Let me look into what went wrong. Do you have the order number and date? Would you like to wait while I research this, or would you prefer I get back to you within the hour?''

4. ''I'm sorry you are dissatisfied with my service. Please tell me specifically what wasn't right so I can correct it. And I'll get Mrs. Hall, my supervisor for you.''

5. ''I can understand how you feel this procedure is a waste of time. I'm sorry, I don't have the authority to complete this transaction differently—only the manager does. When she comes back, I will check to see if I can handle your account differently next time you come in. I'm sorry for the inconvenience today.''

PART 5: AFTER THE CUSTOMER'S GONE

After the customer has left, you may want to take a few minutes for a time out or a cool down. You may need to compose yourself and calm yourself down.

It is important not to focus on what you did poorly. Don't reproach yourself for making mistakes. Instead, use this time to learn how you could handle the situation differently in the future. On the next page is a chart you can photocopy to review what happened.

Incident Review
Don't Take it Personally
Don't Bore Your Coworkers

INCIDENT REVIEW

1. What did I do well in calming this upset customer? (For example: call him/her by name, look him/her in the eye, listen well, want to help, avoid interrupting.)

    _____

    _____

    _____

2. What could I have said that would have calmed him/her better or sooner?

    _____

    _____

    _____

3. What did I say that I don't want to say again?

    _____

    _____

    _____

4. What body language can I use to calm the upset customer better next time?

    _____

    _____

    _____

5. What body language do I want to work on eliminating so it doesn't escalate the upset?

    _____

    _____

    _____

6. What did I learn?

    _____

    _____

    _____

7. Phrases that will help me remember that I am a valuable person and want to be the best I can be:

    I am a valuable person.

    I am working on becoming the best I can be.

    _____

    _____

DON'T TAKE IT PERSONALLY OR BORE YOUR CO-WORKERS

Don't Take it Personally

It is easy to feel that you've been called stupid, when the customer is really upset at the organization, a policy, one of your co-workers, or himself. He is lashing out at whatever is near—in this case, you.

More often than not, his misfortune was not caused by you. You must remind yourself of this. If he says "You screwed up my order" he probably means "My order didn't arrive on time and you people are going to pay for this. Whoever did this is in big trouble, and since I don't know exactly who it is, *you're* going to hear my anger—perhaps you'll put things right."

Sometimes the mistake was your fault. We all make mistakes. It often disarms people if you admit it was your fault and apologize. But only do this if it really was your fault. If you have made this mistake before, ask your boss how you can eliminate the error.

Don't Bore Your Co-Workers

Some people say it helps to get over their own upset if they tell their co-workers about the incident. Ask yourself "Was this a pleasant experience? If not, why would I want to share an unpleasant experience with people I like? Will it help their day go better? Will it make them happier?" The answer is no, it won't make their day happier. So why burden them?

If there is something your co-workers can learn from your experience, then certainly you should share it. For example, you may have learned something about a customer's "hot buttons," because you unknowingly set them off. This information is useful to your co-worker, so he doesn't get into the same hassle with this customer.

You may also want to ask your co-worker for advice. "What would *you* have done?;" "What do you think I should have done?;" "What should I do differently next time?"—these questions can help you learn from the experience.

But if you just want to get it off your chest, don't bother anyone else. Write out the story to yourself. And you can become your own advisor. Ask yourself what you could have done differently.

PART 6: GUIDELINES FOR MANAGERS

How do managers know how customers are being treated? When you aren't around or within earshot, how do you really know how your people are responding to your customers? You don't. You can only rely on your example of customer service to live on through your staff's communication with customers.

As discussed in Part 2, some customers wouldn't have to be calmed if they were not faced with annoyances to begin with. It is critical that you instill customer service concepts in your staff. So let's discuss what managers can do to create an environment conducive to continual customer satisfaction.

Creating an Environment For Customer Satisfaction
Use This Book For A Staff Meeting
When Managers Calm Upset Customers
Managing Upset Employees

CREATING AN ENVIRONMENT FOR CUSTOMER SATISFACTION

Be a role model

You must give more than lip service to the concept of customer satisfaction—you must practice it visibly and frequently. Sending staff to outside courses on customer satisfaction can be a waste of money if the manager does not model and reward good service.

Ask for your staff's suggestions

Your people often have good ideas to improve operations. But some don't feel comfortable making suggestions unless asked.

Use their ideas that make sense. And give credit for them. People resent it when someone else steals their credit.

Solicit customer feedback

There are several inexpensive ways to get feedback:

Postage-paid return cards or surveys

Make sure they're short and to the point. Have a place for the customer to write his/her name and phone number so you can call to clarify any information.

Phone calls

You could personally call five or ten customers each week to check on service. Don't only call customers who you know love your company, but also some who haven't bought from you in a while.

Observe service and ask customers what changes they'd like to see.

CREATING AN ENVIRONMENT (Continued)

Reward good customer-service behavior

When a staff member does a good job, give her immediate feedback. Let her know what the customer said, or what you noticed that showed good service. Be specific: ''I was glad to hear you offer Mrs. Olsen help with her packages.''

Become familiar with the concepts in this book so you can reinforce behavior which calms customers, and counsel your staff when they are behaving in ways that are annoying to customers.

Encourage your staff to use their initiative

Give your staff the authority to act on the customer's behalf. Set a dollar-amount ceiling they can utilize without calling in their supervisor. Increase the ceiling as your trust of the staff member increases. This give him confidence, and allows the customer's problem to be handled immediately, without being bounced around.

In a recent article in *Frequent Flyer*, Paul Auger, vice-president of marketing for Midway Airlines says:

> Employees now have the ability to resolve problems—whatever the problem is—without saying that our policy is ''Write a letter to the president.'' For example, we tell our personnel we're not going to punish them for giving away a free ticket. We counsel them if we feel they're being overzealous. But as long as they feel they're doing it on behalf of the customer, the worst that can happen is that we say, ''Gee, did you really have to go that far?''

Don't talk negatively about customers

''Mrs. Hanson is such a pain in the neck'' teaches nothing. But ''Mrs. Hanson is very detail-oriented. So make sure to check her invoices carefully before you send them out'' explains your concern and what to do about it.

Know when to fire a customer

If a customer continually upsets your staff for trivial reasons, you may need to invite the customer to utilize someone else's services. ''Mr. Pratt, it seems that we cannot meet your expectations for turn-around and acceptable number of rejects. Perhaps it would be better if you found another vendor who could meet your standards.'' Of course, if your organization is a utility, public agency, or government office, this is not an option for you.

USING THIS BOOK FOR A STAFF MEETING

Using this workbook in a staff meeting can help to interest your staff in learning techniques for dealing with customers.

Hand out the books a week or two before your next staff meeting, telling everyone that the topic of the next meeting will be how to calm upset customers.

Make sure you have enough room for everyone at this meeting, as everyone seems interested in this topic.

Each person is responsible for reading the book, completing the exercises, and coming up with ideas on how to adapt the concepts to your group's situations.

When you lead the meeting, become a facilitator, not a dictator. Draw out your staff by asking them open-ended questions about the situations and concepts. Avoid lecturing and pontificating. Even though you are the boss, you will turn everyone off if you tell them that the way *you* handle people is the right and only way.

Some questions you can use in starting the discussion are:

> "Suzanne, share with us your response to question four on page 29 in the "Watch Your Words" practice. Would you elaborate on why you think it's important never to treat a customer the way the staff did in this example?"

> "Blake, how do you think we could adapt _____ here?"

> "What ideas do you have for eliminating things that could annoy our customers?"

Also, have regular discussions at staff meetings about customer service. Give examples of good customer-service behavior as well as problems that may need correcting (don't embarrass anyone). Continually make your concerns and attitude known.

Teach your staff how to learn from negative experiences

Use the questions in the Incident Review sheet in Part 5:

> What did you do well?
> What would you do differently next time?
> What could you do to prevent this from happening again?
> What did you learn?

Evaluate customer-satisfaction performance

Be clear on the minimum levels of customer service you expect. Be specific, e.g.:
  phones to be answered within two rings;
  walk-in visitors greeted within 30 seconds;
  phone calls returned within 4 hours;
  upbeat and helpful behavior;
  smiles when greeting customers.

Let staff members know their performance in these areas will be included in their performance evaluations.

WHEN MANAGERS CALM UPSET CUSTOMERS

The upset customer may be passed to you if your employee can't handle the situation, or if the customer insists on seeing you.

Not only is there an urgent need to calm this customer, your staff are also listening and watching to see how you handle the situation. Remember, you are a role model.

Often the customer will seem calmer and more rational with you than with your staff because you are perceived as having more authority to do something about the problem.

On the other hand, your staff may have done something to escalate the customer's anger. You should be able to handle any situation if you use the guidelines in the first five parts of this book.

What if you blow it?

If you do or say something that annoys the customer further, and you realize your error in retrospect, discuss it at a staff meeting. Explain what you did wrong and either ask the group to suggest a better response, or tell them what you think you should have said or done.

A leader who is willing to admit errors, discuss them, and strategize corrections is a leader that will be respected. Don't be afraid of being vulnerable in front of your staff. If you talk about your mistakes and take action to correct them, you will have the respect of your staff.

MANAGING UPSET EMPLOYEES

During the Incident

Whether she's right or wrong, it's important for you not to make your employee look foolish or incompetent.

If she was right in what she told the customer, say so.

> ''Mrs. Wong, I'm sorry to tell you that your Blue Bird phone service allows you to receive discounts on calls made inside your area code between noon and 2 p.m. As Nancy explained, this is the reason for the calls at 2:08 and 3:32 being charged at the full rate.''

If only you can make an exception to the policy your employee stated, tell the customer so. Emphasize that she was doing her job well.

If the employee was wrong, explain that there must have been a misinterpretation of policy. Emphasize his value in front of the customer.

> ''Yes, Mr. Jones, you are right that you shouldn't be charged for cashiers' checks on your Senior Special account. Obviously, there was a misunderstanding about this. Bill here is one of our finest tellers, so I'm sure it was an oversight. At our next staff meeting I'll remind all our tellers. I'm sorry for your inconvenience. Of course, we'll waive the fee for your cashier's check. Is there anything else we can do for you today?''

After the Customer Has Left

Your employee may be shaken, angry, on the verge of tears. Allow her to retain self-respect and composure in front of her peers and the other customers. Let her take a ten-minute break so she can go to the lounge, restroom, or other quiet place to compose herself.

If at all possible, accompany her and talk to her about the exchange, listen to her vent her anger, and reinforce your support of her actions. When she's calm enough discuss with her how she might handle the situation differently next time. (If she's very upset, postpone the discussion till another time.) Solicit her ideas before telling her yours. The last thing she needs right now is a lecture.

Debriefing the Rest of the Staff

If the rest of the staff heard or saw the incident, it may be appropriate to discuss the scene with them. If it was a serious or physical altercation, debrief them as soon as possible, preferably at the close of that business day or shift. If it was less serious, discuss it at the next staff meeting. Be sure to discuss it with the involved employee beforehand and check whether this would be all right with him or her.

Recap what happened, then focus the discussion on what can be learned: what worked to help calm this customer, and what might be tried differently next time. Don't make negative remarks about the customer's behavior or character.

CUSTOMER SATISFACTION

Customer satisfaction is essential to an organization's survival. Instill the value of this with your staff, recognize their commendable behavior, and teach them to think on behalf of the customer—and you'll have an organization your customers will keep coming back to.

AFFIRM CUSTOMER SATISFACTION
AND YOU'LL BE A WINNER.

PART 7: REVIEW

You now know why it's important to calm upset customers, why customers become upset, what you can do to reduce the chance of upset, how you can calm an upset customer, and what to do after he has left. And if you're a manager, you now know how to create an environment conducive to customer satisfaction.

WHAT DID WE COVER?

Why it is Important to Calm Upset Customers

Because customers are the reason you have a job. They deserve to have their complaints known and, when appropriate, to have something done about them.

You want them to complain because then they are more likely to be loyal to your business. When you respond to their concern promptly and professionally, they will keep coming back—happily.

You can learn from encounters with upset people. You can gain confidence and new insights into yourself and others.

Why Customers Get Upset

Sometimes you may do things that increase customer annoyance and escalate their anger. You can become aware of these behaviors and work at eliminating them.

What You Can Do to Avoid Upsets

Our personal presentation, body language, voice tone, and words all make a difference. If you pay attention to these, you can avoid escalating annoyance into anger.

Calming Upset Customers

You can listen caringly, sincerely, and fully to the customer's concern. You can defuse the customer's defensiveness by using Communication Helpers instead of Fight Starters.

WHAT DID WE COVER (Continued)

What to Do After the Customer's Gone

You can review the interaction to determine what you learned and what you could do differently next time.

What Managers Can Do

You can create an environment conducive to excellent customer service. You can be an outstanding role model by showing your staff continually how you expect customers to be treated. You can reward outstanding service behavior, and treat your employees as you wish them to treat your customers.

NOTES

NOTES

NOTES

NOTES

NOTES

NOTES

NOTES

OVER 150 BOOKS AND 35 VIDEOS AVAILABLE IN THE 50-MINUTE SERIES

We hope you enjoyed this book. If so, we have good news for you. This title is part of the best-selling *50-MINUTE*™ *Series* of books. All *Series* books are similar in size and identical in price. Many are supported with training videos.

To order *50-MINUTE* Books and Videos or request a free catalog, contact your local distributor or Crisp Publications, Inc., 1200 Hamilton Court, Menlo Park, CA 94025. Our toll-free number is (800) 442-7477.

50-Minute Series Books and Videos Subject Areas . . .

Management
Training
Human Resources
Customer Service and Sales Training
Communications
Small Business and Financial Planning
Creativity
Personal Development
Wellness
Adult Literacy and Learning
Career, Retirement and Life Planning

Other titles available from Crisp Publications in these categories

Crisp Computer Series
The Crisp Small Business & Entrepreneurship Series
Quick Read Series
Management
Personal Development
Retirement Planning